Erotic Conundrums
At Ease Press
ISBN   978-1-105-79997-6

Text by James H. Burleson
Edited by Carl Callaway
Cover: *La nascita di Venere*, Sandro Botticelli (1445 – 1510)
Published by ateasepress.com
Revised December 15, 2016

ISBN   978-1-105-79997-6

Erotic Conundrums
from Sulpicia to Sappho

English Versions of Latin and Greek Poetry

James H. Burleson

Edited by Carl Callaway

For my Mother Faye, who gave me life

Contents

De Rerum Natura

I.1-20

Lucretius

~99 – ~55 BCE

Hymn to Venus

Progenetrix of Aeneas' race, Pleasure of Gods and Mortals,
Venus our Source, who crowd the ship-bearing Sea
with teeming life beneath the gliding constellations
and animate the Earth prodigious-with-fruit,
through you is each species of living creatures conceived
and borne forth to behold the splendid Sun.
You, Goddess, truly the Winds curl back from you;
the Clouds withdraw for your descent;
ingenious Earth shoots up soft blooms to greet you;
Ocean becalms his billows and smiles toward you;
tranquil Sky outpours his radiant light upon you.
For, just when Day's countenance begins to green
and West Wind's generative thrust, set free, blows boldly,
first the birds on high begin to note you, Goddess,
as you approach, and your power infuses their hearts.
Then the beasts both wild and tame
start bounding across the exuberant meadows
or swimming the coursing streams.
Thus o'ertaken by your charm,
each sportive creature follows wherever you lead.
Finally, throughout all seas and mountains
and rapacious rivers and frondiferous havens of birds
and lavish green fields you incite seductive Amor
to pierce the hearts of creatures one and all,
arousing their lust to procreate, each according to its kind.

Preface

Following are my English versions of Latin and Greek poems. Special thanks are due to my loyal friend Morris Fry for patiently correcting some of my gongorisms across the years.

Roman poets frequently expressed the idea of the brevity of life and the logic of enjoying it while it could be enjoyed. Many of them were receptive to the Epicurean principle that the goal of life is *voluptas*, pleasure, personified as Venus, Goddess of Love: Pleasure of Gods and Mortals; smiling, happy, erotic, arousing, laughterloving Venus, who infuses the hearts of all creatures, according to Lucretius, with a lust to procreate; Venus, the mother of Cupid (or *Eros* or *Amor*). Precisely because this desire is irresistible, Venus was called the cruelest of gods, for life often raises barriers to love's fulfillment. Hence my title Erotic Conundrums. Socrates lends understanding to this tantalizing aspect of Eros in Plato's *Symposium*, where he points out that Eros itself can only be the lack of the object desired.

The pieces of this collection move generally backward in time, from *levitas* and Romanticism steadily into deeper *gravitas* and Classicism.

Tibullus and Sulpicia

Albius Tibullus lived from 54 to 19 BCE. Two books of his elegies were published in about 19, and at an indefinite time another book was subsequently appended. Five poems from the third book are of uncertain authorship and are called The Garland of Sulpicia. She is thought to have been a relative of Messalla Corvinus, a general and the patron of Tibullus. These elegies, written by or about her, concern her lover Cerinthus. In this one, III.9, she coquettishly attempts to attract him home from a hunting trip, that is to say, from his devotion to Diana, Goddess of Hunting, back to Venus. I have composed lines 5 and 6, evidently missing from the manuscripts.

The poet's form is elegiac couplet; I have used trochaic alternating with iambic lines. The poet is coquettish.The mood is peevishly seductive. The lover is Cerinthus. The conundrum is Absent Lover.

Elegy III.9

de Sulpicia

from Book III of Tibullus,
added to his first two books after publication
~ 19 BCE

Venus versus Venery

Spare my sweetheart, javelina, where you wander
    afield, through pastures green or mountain-thickets dim.
Whet your hardy tusks, yet not to spar with him, sir.
    Love, be his guardian; return him safe to me.
Holy Venus made our bond of light, with Cupid.
    So bright a mortal union might no more occur;

but, Diana led him off afar a-hunting.
    I damn the forest, scoff the boring, barking hounds.
Fond, obsessed, he lacerates his gentle hands, when
    the bounds are circled 'round on slanting, dense terrain:
into lairs of animals he creeps. Amusing.
    I scorn abusing fair white limbs on brier thorns.

Fine, Cerinthus, if I too may come there with you
    to bear the twisted net across the hills myself;
mine to trail the prey; I'll track the fleeting stag and
    set free the eager dogs – their metal collars loose.
Then the woods would please me, o my light, if we could
    make love beneath the net. May thus be known the truth.

Let wild boar come forth but safely leave us nesting,
    lest he, uncouth, annoy us savoring our joy.
May no Venus chase with you but me alone; for
    Diana rules – the unchaste may not hunt, pure boy.
Whosoever other dares to snare my lover
    let cruel beasts attack and savage her to shreds.

Leave this mad desire for hunting to your sire, and
    make haste, I pray; come back to my embrace, to bed.

Notes:

1. The following is a Latin version of lines 5 and 6, supplied by the author to fill a presumed lacuna.

Nos Venus in nexum dea iunxere atque Cupido;
   clarior haud hominum iunctio ea fuerit.

2. The common names wild boar and javelina, classified respectively *Sus scrofa* and *Peccari angularis*, are casually confused in the Southwest of the United States.

Ovid

Publius Ovidius Naso, Ovid, lived from 43 BCE to 18 CE. This selection, written ~1 BCE, is Poem 7 from Book III of his *Amores,* Love-affairs. Because of such indiscrete publications and because of his behavior regarding the Emperor Augustus' daughter, Ovid came into conflict with an element of Augustus' program, that of restoring pristine Roman morality; and he, the most urbane of poets, was consequently exiled to the edge of the Black Sea. You will understand why momentarily. This piece concerns an episode of impotence on Ovid's part; but, typically, there is an Ovidian coda, which this remark of Wolfgang Mozart (in a letter to his wife) may be taken to foreshadow:

> As I write, he is crawling onto the table and looking at me questioningly.... I can hardly keep the villain in his place.

Ovid's form is elegiac couplet; I have used iambic pentameter. The poet is urbane and conversational. The mood is self-effacing and comic. The lover is unnamed but eager. The conundrum is Impotence.

Amores III.7

Ovid

43 BCE – 18 CE

Phallusie

For M.F.

"No stunning fox," of her I might have said,
"not quite refined, nor object of my prayer,"
since I lay impotent with her, and bare,
a shameful burden on a sluggard bed.

What longing! But could we enjoy it? No.
This torpid miser hoarded our delight.
She hugged me hard about the neck, more white
her arms of ivory than highland snow.

Her eager kiss and tongue embroidered lust;
she intertwined my upper legs with her;
she asked what else I wished and called me sir
and purred endearing words for me to trust.

My lazy little man stayed cool – as still
as wooden flute – and foiled my thrust-of-will.

I lay there like a stump or useless clown,
uncertain whether I were man or ghost.
What then, if anything, will old-age boast,
if youth itself in all its pride falls down?

The shame: my youth and manhood lost so soon;
the lady had me not as boy or man,
but rose as Vestal Virgin flames to fan,
or sister merely graced by brother's boon.

Last week I had blonde Clytie twice, and right
fair Pytho thrice, and Libby thrice, as well;
and I recall, last Summer, hot as Hell,
Corrinna scored nine times with me one night.

There must have been some spell or toxic trick
that someone wrought to paralyze my ****.

A witch affixed my name to doll of wax?
As pins impale its liver, passions die.
Enchantment makes a flowing spring run dry,
and curses turn the fields of wheat to grass.

A holm-oak's acorns drop when hexed; the grape –
all fruits when charmed are shed without a breeze.
If magic casts a damning spell on these,
might it as well bedroop my vector-shape?

My shame looms over me once more; its pain,
another cause for my deficiency.
I touched her only where the eyes may see,
where tunic lightly brushes surface-plane.

Her touch would render Nestor young again,
Tithonus studlier than he has been.

She lay against me, no man, it would seem.
What prayer or novel vow must I invent?
I think the gods are sorry that they sent
so fine a gift, dysused by one so mean.

I craved for her to want me and to dole
me kisses and to squeeze me. This came true.
Though luck and power fell to me, I rue
last night when my libido failed their goal.

To thirst in river's midst, with fruit at hand
to starve are gossips' just rewards, I'm sure.
Yet who could leave this angel's bed so pure
and face the gods, who would not understand?

Her best seductive kisses went to waste
with all attempts to gratify my taste.

Her ways could quicken steel or marble block
or raise an oaken log without travail.
She has the stuff to stir the living male;
no longer live or male, myself I mock.

The highest tenor cannot soothe the deaf;
the brightest painting can't delight the blind.
What happy dreams I'd made within my mind;
what plans I'd laid successively to F.!

Still, there he lay, like one about to die,
more languid than a rose plucked yesterday.
Behold, he rises now – untimely, *très
puissant*! Call cohorts out: the chase is nigh!

Why not play shy again, you impish bore?
Your promise doomed me rudely once before.

When you betrayed your master, caught unarmed,
I wore pathetic, sore embarrassment.
My lady held no scorn by then and lent
an easy hand to squeeze you forth unharmed;

but, when she saw, in spite of all her wiles,
your heedless disinclinedness, she said:
"Unwilling tease, to bring this stunt to bed –
you madman, who has dared you, just for smiles?

Some hag in woolen cowl bewitched your chode,
or you and someone else have worn it out!"
With tunic held in front for her dismount,
and rightly barefoot, off she spritely strode.

Anon, to keep the maid from her disgrace,
she stained the sheet with water from a vase.

Horace

Soon after the assassination of Julius Caesar in 44, Octavian (who would be named Augustus by the Roman senate in 27), began to consolidate his control of the Roman government. Through the ensuing years he developed a program of peace, prosperity, and the promotion of traditional Roman values, through legislation and support of the arts. He evidently conceived all elements of his program to be mutually reinforcing. An integral part of his support for literature was the establishment of Greek and Latin libraries at Rome. Both Horace and Vergil were friends of Augustus; and they were both nurtured in the circle of the Etruscan Maecenas, who served without title as Minister of Culture and Secretary of State for the Emperor. Like Vergil, Horace gratefully received a sinecure from the regime.

Quintus Horatius Flaccus, Horace, lived from 65 to 8 BCE. In his lyric poetry Horace combined Stoic *virtus* (excellence) with Epicurean *voluptas* (pleasure). His great pride was to have brought the old Greek meters to life again in Latin. His meticulous compositions, Nietzsche said, were like the fine art of mosaic.

Book IV of Horace's *Carmina* was published at Augustus' behest in ~13 BCE, some ten years after the first three. These later lyric poems, more authentically personal, often demonstrate a deepened maturity of thought.

In *Carmina* IV.1 Horace avers that his advancing age has inured him to Venus' charms. He prays for her to spare him from more of love's conflicts; besides, he has had ample fulfillment in his younger days. She should find a receptive subject, one who will spare no cost to honor her in return. Horace seems carefree and confident as he creates his poem.

Then in the final stanzas comes a serious mood swing, for Venus insinuates her power after all, into Horace's subconscious mind – into his dreams, yet he finds his resultant love unrequited. Thus the poet is spared from a lover but not from desire. A direct view of the dysphoria that now besets him is that it arose, given his conscious denial of erotic interest, from the revelation in his dreams that though love may flee age, the reverse may not be possible.

If we listen closely, the poet suggests further ironies with exquisite subtlety. From Horace's muted nostalgia for his youthful affairs proceeds the genius of this poem: the poignancy of a final fleeting phantom of love, which by vanishing even from his dreams leaves the poet void of all emotions save despair, and void of his creative gift as well – for the heart of lyric poetry is love. He is to be left silent and alone with his despondency. His overt plea was for Venus to spare him from love; his tacit plea at the poem's close is for her to restore the beloved to him. Venus has given Horace an inescapable yet unattainable love. This ironic fulfillment of his conscious wish – the lover has vanished – brings him only emptiness. This outcome tacitly implies a punishment by Venus, in spite of his elaborate vision for her honors, for his rejection of her *numen*. Venus may not be dismissed.

Surely Horace had recalled a parallel to this manifestation of Venus' ironic and pervasive power, in Venus' words from Sappho's *Ode to Aphrodite* (fragment 1):

> Yea, for if now he shun, he soon shall chase thee;
> Yea, if he loved not, soon shall he begin to
> Love thee, unwilling.
>
> [tr. John Addington Symonds]

Horace's meter is Second Asclepiadean, which I have imitated. The poet's mood is confident nonchalance, then poignant wistfulness. The lover is Ligurinus. The conundrum is Unrequited Love in Dreams.

Carmina IV.1

Horace

65 – 8 BCE

Plea to Venus

Would you now reignite a war
long-cooled, Venus? O spare me, this I pray you, please.
I'm no longer the man I was
when warm Cinara ruled over me. Cease to force,

o harsh Mother of all hot loves,
me, hard-hearted by now, fifty years old, about,
back to blandishing Love's command.
Go where youth call you, where naturally they pray.

You'll find ample success and more,
if your revels approach Maximus Paulus' house.
Fly there, winged on your crimson swans,
should you wish to enfire his ripe, receptive heart.

This young man is genteel and buff,
not nonplussed at the bar, anxious defendants' star.
Well-rehearsed in a hundred ploys,
this lad will bear the flag over your army, far.

Smile he will, as the more endowed,
on each rival, whose rich gifts garner no reward.
Your fine form he'll in marble set,
near that lake to the North, under a cedarn roof.

There much incense will constantly
burn for you to inhale; flutes sent from Phrygia,
lyres' soft strings, and the shepherds' pipes
will in harmony blend music for your delight.

Twice each day will a rite display,
there for you, by your shrine, delicate boys and girls,
barefoot, striking the ground in dance,
while they hymn your divine force, like our noble priests.

No lad, lady, or hope naïve
toward some mutual bond has any chance to please
me at my age, nor wine in bouts,
nor fresh flowers in wreaths fastened around my brow.

Yet, my god, Ligurinus, why?
Why start teardrops adown, one at a time, my face?
Why falls silent my eloquent
voice, so awkwardly, 'mid words so articulate?

While I sleep, through my dreams you pass:
you, though held fast-embraced, flee; I pursue in vain
you fleet-flying across Mars' Field,
you hard-hearted away slipping through swirling streams.

This poem was published in 23 BCE with Horace's first three books of Songs. It is *Carmen* III.I2, the Neobule Ode. In it we hear subliminal echoes of Castor, Pollux, Meleager, Hercules, Hyas, Odysseus, Adonis, and Amphion. The poem is thus like a painting replete with faces only partially revealed. Here, as in the elegy of Sulpicia, we find that the terms of love are dictated more by Diana than by Venus; Minerva, the Goddess of Weaving, also exerts control in the beginning. For, as all well-bred Roman women, even those of Augustus' family, were by custom devoted to her, so Neobule, who must spend her days indoors, spinning her quota of wool and weaving cloth from it. She meanwhile pines for a young man, an athlete and hunter whom she has seen or imagined. Though some have termed this piece a soliloquy, the poet speaks of her, then to her; and then the young lady herself, taken away into a dream-like state, muses on the physique and prowess of the young man. This short piece has an uncertain outcome, and Neobule may have to make a New Plan (her name from the Greek).

Horace's meter is Ionic *a minore*, which I have imitated. The poet is omniscient. The mood is one of poignant longing. The lover is Hebrus. The conundrum is Fantasy Lover.

Carmina III.12

Horace

65 – 8 BCE

New Plan

There is no joy for the young lady who can't daydream of romance
or allay worries with sweet wine, not without fear that her guardian
then would scold her to despondence.

Does the boy-god, son of soft Venus, wing off all your devotion
to Minerva, hide your wool-basket and loom now, Neobule,
in the bright aura of Hebrus,

Liparaean? "See his oiled shoulders; he swims over the Tiber;
more a horseman than Bellerophon, unbowed boxer, a victor
unexcelled running the race-course,

in the chase cunning: o'er field javelin flies straight toward a fleet stag
as the herd starts; then he darts into the dense brush where the prize catch,
for his spear match, waits, a wild boar."

Vergil

Publius Vergilius Maro lived from 70 to 19 BCE. His four books of *Georgics*, Song of the Earth-Workers, were written between ~36 and ~29, and the first edition was published in ~29. These nominally didactic compositions, on agronomy, animal husbandry, arboriculture, and apiculture, were written at the behest of Maecenas; for Augustus' program, conceived at the close of a hundred-year span of civil strife and wars that had devastated the population and productivity of Italy, included the goal of restored prosperity for all Italy. The motivation of citizens to establish themselves on farms or ranches, to sustain themselves on the land through enterprise and productive labor, as most Italians had done in earlier times, was a significant element of this goal.

The first half of Book IV teaches the art of beekeeping: here the writing is instructive or descriptive or at times ethnographical, that is, the bees' polity and way of life are often comparable with those of human culture.

The following passage is from the second half, an epyllion, Vergil's myth of Aristaeus. His story exemplifies the very pursuits that the four books of *Georgics* inculcate. Aristaeus, however, is struck with passion for the Dryads' companion Eurydice, the wife of his cousin Orpheus. Eurydice runs from Aristaeus as fast as she can, but treads on a viper in the grass, dies, and goes down to the Underworld. There Orpheus follows, unwilling to give her up. He charms Proserpina and Dis, Queen and King of Hell, with lyre and song. They allow him to lead Eurydice back to life – with one proviso: he must not look back upon her until she emerges from the infernal realm.

Aristaeus, unaware of the consequences from his pursuit of Eurydice, meanwhile is mystified and distraught upon the death of his beloved bees. He goes to the River Peneus to seek a solution from his mother, the Naiad Cyrene. He descends to her cave beneath the river, where she tells him that he must seek an oracle from her grandmother's cousin Proteus, a blue and ancient Sea-God with the abilities to prophesy and to shift his shape. The oracle, we find, is the story of Orpheus.

Vergil's meter is dactylic hexameter; mine is iambic pentameter. The poet is mystic. The mood is pastoral. The lover is Eurydice. The conundrums are A Lover Running Away As Fast As Possible and A Lover In Hell.

from *Georgics* IV

Vergil

70 – 19 BCE

The Oracle of Proteus

Cyrene bade the river part a space,
enough for his descent to the abyss.
So back the river bowed from him; concave,
a wall of water welcomed him within.
He saw his mother's dripping world, amazed
at lakes enclosed in caves and roiling groves;
astonished by their torrents' mighty force,
beneath the Earth he watched the rivers course:
Caïcus, Phasis, Lycus, Anio,
the spring where deep Enipeus' jets surge forth,
the fount whence Father Tiberinus pours,
the Hypanis who 'round big boulders roars,
Eridanus, the bull with gilded horns,
than whom no other River-God could chute
more wildly through his plowed and fruitful bournes
to meet the Sea and disappear in blue.
As Aristaeus passed into her cave
beneath its glassy dome of pumice rock,
wherein Cyrene's regal couch is placed,
she knew how reft of empty tears he was.
Her sister-Nymphs spilled forth abundant drops
of lucid spring-drawn water for his hands
and furnished cloths, then alternately topped
the flagons, laid the table, or they fanned
the altar, burning frankincense to waft.

"Now lift your draft of Lydian," she said.
"To Ocean offer due libations. Pour."
Invoking him, of all the Father, then
two hundred sisters – Dryads watching o'er
the forests, Naiads plying riverbeds –
she steamed the hearth with nectar three times more.
Three times the flames against the ceiling ran.
With this propitious omen she began.
"The azure priest of Neptune, Proteus,
abides around Scarpanto in the Sea.
Now dolphin yoked with hippocampus pull
his chariot across the broad and deep
toward Pallen', his home, and Thessaly.
We Nymphs and ageless Nereus himself
revere him, lo, a wizard knowing all.
What is and was and soon will be he tells.
He holds the herds of Neptune in his thrall
and feeds these slimy seals submarinal.
At first he must be caught by you, my son,
and held in fetters, forced to yield the cause
of illness whence your bees were all undone,
and then to bless whatever next befalls;
for otherwise no oracle will come.

To beg is futile. Never will he bend.
So hold him tightly chained. His tricks will fail.
Now I myself, as soon as Sun ascends
the height of noon, when Summer renders frail
the thirsty verdure urging sheep to seek
the shade, will lead you near his secret vale,
wherein the wearied Ancient One retreats
to rest from faring over Ocean's pale,
where you will reach him easily in sleep;
but, when you have him really fast-enchained,
he'll morph from form to form: this twin of beasts
becomes a prickly boar, a tiger-fiend,
a scaly snake, a lion yellow-maned;
he'll howl the scathing sound of fire; then,
if captive yet, with shapeless water blent,
he'll slip your stays and seaward slide again.
The more he changes shape, more tightly turn
the chains around him, child, till he relearns
the human form you found asleep at first."
She ceased to speak and spilled ambrosial scent
for his anointment; over him it went.
How sweet the breath of air that wreathed his hair;
rebounded now his strength and *savoir-faire*.

Below a certain hollow mountain-face
a spacious cavern opens on the Sea.
Here wind-blown tides flow in and out or stay
as placid pools inside – tranquillity
for storm-tossed sailors lost upon the beach,
till Proteus arrives to claim his cave,
where he betimes behind a boulder sleeps.
As Sirius arises in the sky,
imparting ardent searing Summertime,
the thirsty Ethiopians to dry,
our Nymph brings Aristaeus near to hide
within a covert shielded from the light,
while she herself retires far away
to watch him through a camouflaging haze.
The blazing Sun is gazing straight above
upon the withered foliage below.
His rays are baking rivers into mud,
as Proteus toward his grotto goes
amid the sportive creatures of the Sea,
displacing salty spray as they careen.
Then sleep his pod of seals upon the strand;
and he, as would a shepherd on a height,
when Vesper brings the bullocks from the land
and pleading lambs the famished wolves invite,
sits down upon a crag to count his band.
Anon to Aristaeus comes his chance:
no sooner lies the magus down to rest
than, suddenly and loudly manifest,
Lord Aristaeus manacles his hands.
The sorcerer invokes his magic art
to change miraculously form to form,
wild beast to raging flood to fire-storm;
but none of these allows him to depart.
So Proteus takes human form once more,
and using human language he implores:

"Who then are you, most impudent of youths,
to raid my cave? Who is it you obey?
What do you wish?" To him is answer made:
"Since nothing fools you, sayer of the sooth,
who know what happens – present, future, past –
your wise deceitful lies must cease at last.
I follow Gods' divine direction where
an oracle may mend collapsed affairs."
Thus Aristaeus captures him by force.
His luminescent eyes transfix this lord,
while through his gnashing teeth the Fates sing forth:

"Infernal wrath averts your path, and bold
the sin you will atone to Orpheus,
for grief would wreak its toll (not what you owe;
nay, less – the Fates finessed him), since you took
his wife away; and he is truly wroth.
She wildly fleeing you to water hied.
Her doom: a massive hiding viper eyed
her path along his grassy riverside.
The sister-Dryads cried; the mountain-heights
repined; their sad reply from citadels
of tall Pangaea and Rhodope rained;
the Hebrus mourned; the Getae wept as well –
yes, all of Mars' aggressive land of Thrace;
and tears from Attic Orithyia fell.
Poor Orpheus consoled his broken heart:
he played his lyre made of tortoise shell
alone along the shore from dawn to dark
and sang for you, his precious wife in Hell.
Then live into the maw of Hades bound,
he stalked beneath the gates of Dis; profound
and fearful fog this dismal grove surrounds.
Then phantom shades appeared; he saw the King
of Horrors – hard whose heart had ceded naught
to human cares or prayers. He thought to sing
would soften Orcus' haughtiness, if aught.
The depths of Erebus sent up their dead,
mere looming airy lightless likenesses
in gloomy multitudes by music led,

as many as the myriads of birds
that wing to leafy shelter ere the night
should fall; as, when a Winter shower bursts
upon the hills, they all arise in flight:
of mothers, husbands – shapes devoid of life –
brave heroes hale of heart before they died,
unmarried maidens, boys without a wife,
whose pyres once had seared their sires' eyes.
Cocytus slurried mud as black as pitch,
that held the dead in dense and ragged reeds –
a loathsome swamp of stagnant water. Styx
imprisoned Hell in nine concentric streams.
All Tartarus emerged from inner rooms;
came Furies, hair in serpents arch and blue;
astonished stood the spectral House of Doom;
Ixion on his wheel no longer flew;
and Cerberus allowed three jaws to droop.
Eurydice was won. They bounded up
to fairer air. Pursued, he led the way
around each pitfall; out he vaulted; but,
impulsive folly conquered love's delay.
The shades had shriven him, if any could.
Proserpina's proviso, though, was law.
Without a thought he broke it, for he looked
behind and saw her bathed in light – the flaw
that laid his labor waste; so he forsook
the hope his deal with brutal Dis had brought.

As Lake Avernus quaked with thunder thrice,
'What catastrophic madness forced our loss
each one from each, my Orpheus?' she cried.
'Behold, the Fates atrociously recall
my name above but downward draw my life.
Not yours, I lift weak hands to you. They fall.
My swimming eyes are dimming. Now I faint.
Be strong. All-veiling Night fades me away.'
She spoke and vanished instantly from sight –
as mist dispersed in wind; nor had she spied
him last – he'd grasped her ghost, or vainly tried,
but swallowed back the words of his reply.
When Charon, Orcus' ferryman, forbade
his crossing yet again the miry bog,
he pondered what to do and where to take
himself; his wife had twice been carried off.
'Again to bend the mystic will of Hell?'
he thought. 'Could tearful lyrics warm a ghost?'
Afloat upon the Styx and cold in death
she was indeed, on Charon's narrow boat.
They say for seven months the poet wept
by lofty cliffs where River Strymon flows;
and there or down in caves of ice he kept,
and told his life in all that he composed.
And as he sang, the tigers' hearts were calm,
while oaks discretely gathered 'round his psalm.

Thus nightingale in veiling poplar keens
for fallen small ones, by a farmer seen
full-feathered Philomelae yet to be,
but rudely dashed to ground with nest and tree.
Upon a limb, to fill the night she weeps
her song in plaintive timbres, then repeats
her haunting melody for those she seeks.
No thought to love or wed would stop his plans
alone to wander icy Arctic lands,
to compass Tanaïs in snow, to cross
Rhipaean fields of ever-present frost,
to mourn Eurydice forever lost,
sure gift of Dis, returned at such a cost.
The Thracian Bacchants took this for his scorn
and loosed their wrath on Orpheus one night:
he limb from youthful limb was cruelly torn
and strewn across the fields amid the rites
of all the Gods, to Bacchus sacrificed;
they disconnected head from sculpted neck
and flung it on the River Hebrus; rolled
along his father's waters, speaking yet,
with waning breath and tongue already cold,
'My poor Eurydice, alas,' it said.
The river echoed back from banks to bed."
When Proteus had finished with his speech,
he whirled and arched and dove into the deep.
His vortex turned to foam beneath the Sea.

Vergil's Bucolics, the ten *Eclogues*, were written between ~42 and ~35 BCE. It was this set of poems that brought Vergil's genius to the attention of Maecenas and thus to Octavian just as he began to formulate his program. Future commissioned works resulted, which supported this program and immortalized Vergil's fame.

Eclogues II took inspiration primarily from another Hellenistic poet, Theokritos, who in his eleventh *Idyll* depicted a futile erotic pursuit, the Cyclops Polyphemus' pursuit of the Nymph Galatea. [See also Ovid's *Metamorphoses* XIII.] Vergil was to employ the theme again, in *Georgics* IV: Aristaeus' pursuit of Eurydice. Beyond informing the central story-line of this *Eclogue*, the theme echoes subliminally throughout. For example, though his myth is not elaborated, mere reference to the god Pan calls to mind his pursuit of the Nymph Syrinx, from whose metamorphosis came the Pan-pipe. [See Ovid's *Metamorphoses* I, and hear Debussy's *Syrinx* for solo flute.] Another example: the single word *lauri* evokes Apollo's pursuit of the Nymph Daphne and her resultant metamorphosis into the laurel tree. [See Ovid's *Metamorphoses* I.]

Here, the shepherd Corydon relates his futile pursuit of the young house-servant Alexis. Every possible enticement of country life is offered him, but still Alexis runs away. Corydon spends a scorching Summer's afternoon in composing the "artless" shreds of this blandishing love-song.

Other shepherds and servants are named and sometimes mocked, including the fair Amaryllis, formerly, it is hinted, in *liaison* with Corydon. To the end of his song he remains adamant for Alexis while simultaneously aware of his own futility, which he also mocks. His percept of incipient madness due to his futile attraction, compounded by the blazing heat of the Sun, reminds us of the first *Idyll*, where Theokritos noted Aphrodite, "ever accursed to all humankind". Vergil suggests here, as elsewhere, that *Amor* usurps the energy necessary for one's labor; also, *Amor* may not only drive the lover mad but may even bring about his/her death. [For Dido's fatal attraction, see *Aeneid* IV.] Yet within its aura of futility this poem is all airy lightness.

Such ironies abound in *Eclogues* II. If we read carefully, we find that Corydon does not, as he claims, stalk Alexis in the tedious sunshine, but rests ensconced in the cool shade of the beech trees. He is not singing directly to Alexis as he implies, for only the trees and hills hear his song. Alexis has already fled away. Though Corydon has viewed his own aging reflection and at one point mocks himself as a "boor" for his futile wishes, his poignancy is ultimately betrayed at the poem's close by an almost aristocratic imperturbability. For then Corydon suddenly resumes his work and wonders who's next. Our uncouth shepherd, we find, knows Greek poetry; his labor of composition, thence derived, along with his other labors, seems to have cured his love-sickness. One suspects that he has been all along, as he is at the end, *sans-souci*.

Vergil's meter is dactylic hexameter, which I have imitated. The poet is whimsical and ironic. The mood is self-effacing and seductive. The lover is Alexis. The conundrum is Unrequited Love.

Eclogues II

Vergil

70 – 19 BCE

Sun, I'm Done

Shepherd and bard, Corydon burned with love for the handsome Alexis.
Dove of their master was he. Corydon thus could not have his wishes.
Deep was the shade where the tall, thick beech trees made him his own place.
There, all alone, he would sing out his songs. Though artless, their verses
echoed his ardent but hollow obsession. The forested hills heard:

"Heartless Alexi, o why do you deem all my songs so unworthy?
Have you no mercy for love? You will force me to lie in the Earth soon.

Scorching, the noon-Sun. The sheep rest cool past the edge of the shadows.
Even the green-hued lizards have sheltered, under the thorn-hedge.
Thestylis must be compounding her herbs now, garlic with wild thyme:
fare aromatic, repast for sere reapers' retreat from severe heat.
I yet follow your footprints, as woods on the mountains resound with
locusts' monotonous droning, and mine, in the tedious Sunshine.

I had done better to suffer the moods of my fair Amaryllis –
rude her disdain supercilious, cruel her temper mercurial –
quite – or in spite of your hue, lily-white, to seduce dark Menalcas.
Winsome friend, one must never depend on the color of one's skin:
privets' white blooms wilt soon, but hyacinths last when they're gathered.

You must abhor me, Alexi; you surely ignore my existence.
How rich in flocks am I, stocked always with bountiful fresh milk;
I tend a thousand lambs that graze these Sicilian mountains;
I lack milk white as new snow neither in Summer nor Winter;
I'll sing you ballads of old, those Theban Amphion sang for
calling his cattle along toward home, down Mount Aracynthus.

Close to the Ocean-shore in the shallows, tranquil as winds stilled,
not long ago my reflection astounded me – not yet too worn-out;
so I won't mind if you match me to Daphnis, if images don't lie.

You will be happy: o merely come live here with me near the pastures.
Home may be humble, but we shall be hunters, impaling the great stags.
Goats we shall herd with our staffs, made of long green stalks of hibiscus.
Pan's own song you will mime on the Pan-pipe, with me, in the woodland.
Pan first invented our craft by combining some reeds sealed with bees' wax.
Pan on high keeps watch on the flocks and protects us, the shepherds.
No need for you to lament first attempts, lips spent on the reed-tips.
What was Amyntas unwilling to do for his lessons in Pan-pipe?
My pipe, fashioned of seven unequal reed-stems of hemlock,
was old Damoetas' before. On his deathbed he gave it to me, and
"This thing will play you next," he said, our Damoetas, the shepherd.
Foolish Amyntas envied the gift and the art of the Pan-pipe.

Also I have two roebucks, saved from a perilous canyon;
dappled their coats yet with patches of white; each morning and evening
they nurse a ewe dry – two at a time; and for you, lad, I keep them.
Thestylis always begs me to let her lead them away, so
take them she will, since my gifts seem to you too rustic and mundane.

Run here to me, o my handsome lad: lo, Nymphs come to meet us;
baskets brimming with lilies they bring you; a radiant Naiad
also regales you, with light-fringed violets, poppies' red flowers,
garlands of cinnamon, anise, narcissus – cascades of their fragrance,
hyacinth-clusters entwined with sweet herbs midst marigolds' luster.
Now I myself shall pick you some quinces covered in white down,
then brown chestnuts, such as my friend loved, the fair Amaryllis.
Plums – they're as supple as wax – add the crown to this wreath from the fruit trees;
for it I'll harvest first you, o laurels, and next you, o myrtle:
woven together you blend so well your mellow aromas.

You play the boor, Corydon, since Alexis disdains what you offer.
Aye, Lord Iollas assuredly would win a contest of presents.
Sad, the estate that, alas, Fate has granted to me for my wishes:
mindlessly have I admitted the South Wind to ravish my flowers;
coarse wild boars now cavort in the ponds, once calm, 'round my fountains.

Whom do you thoughtlessly flee? Gods also have dwelled in the wildwood.
Paris of Troy has, as well. Let Pallas abide in her city.
O, may the greenwood enthrall us more fully than all things beside could.

Violent lioness stalks lean wolf; he, in hunger, young she-goat;
frolicsome goat hunts for blossoms of clover; likewise I follow
you, o Alexi, my boy. Each unique joy calls forth its creature.

Look, how the bullocks are bearing the plowshare home on their yoke-beam;
now, as the Sunset doubles the span of the shadows, the Night comes.
Love yet consumes me. How will I quell it? Nothing will cool love.

Ah, what has dazed me? Malaise? Am I crazy, undone by the hot Sun?
I have abandoned the grapevines half-pruned on elm trees in dense leaf.
Ere day's end I may still do something of use and with real skill....
Ply damp rushes with switches of willow into a basket?

If this Alexis rejects me, I next will discover another."

Sappho

Orpheus, whose myth we heard above and to whom much early poetry and pre-Socratic cosmology were actually attributed, is a link to Pythagoras, to his doctrine of reincarnation, and thus to Plato. The Hebrus River in Thrace, down which Orpheus' head floated, recalls Hebrus in the Neobule Ode; the river carried the head to the island of Lesbos, where it was said to have continued to prophesy for years in a cave sacred to Dionysus. And it was on Lesbos that the finest Greek lyric poet later lived and loved, the poet Sappho.

Psappho flourished ~600 BCE. Her own circle, called a *thiasos*, was composed of young women who came to her before their time of marriage. Plato deified Sappho as The Tenth Muse. Werner Jaeger wrote:

> No masculine love poetry among the Greeks even
> approached the spiritual depths of Sappho's lyrics.

In this poem we hear of a violet crown. Until perhaps a half century ago, The Violet Crown was an alternate name for this city and was used in a story by O. Henry; it was derived from the corona of violet light that sometimes encircles and settles softly upon the horizon of Austin at sunset.

Sappho's meter in this fragment is an Aeolic variant, which I have imitated. The poet is noble. The mood is despondency masked by nobility. The lover is unnamed. The conundrum is Lover Departing Reluctantly.

Fragment 94

Sappho

floruit ~ 600 BCE

I'm not lying. I long to die.
Tears streamed down from her eyes ere she had to fly.

This she often repeated: "All's
lost – such awful events befall
us, my Sappho. I hate to abandon you."

Thus my answer: "Recall me, dear.
Go; be cheerful. Though far from here,
always hold in your heart how we cherished you.

One wish only, to bring to mind,
lest you ever forget, the fine
soft things, those we alone once shared awhile.

Oft bright wreaths graced your hair, as you,
rosebud- , crocus- , and violet-crowned,
lay near me as we lingered upon our couch.

Blooms I plaited for you to wear,
garlands draped 'round your neck so fair,
fragrant delicate plights of our tender love.

Myrrh reserved for a queen you spread,
though dear, freely upon my head....
Then your longing was sated, and soft our bed."

www.ingramcontent.com/pod-product-compliance
Lightning Source LLC
LaVergne TN
LVHW011410080426
835511LV00005B/465